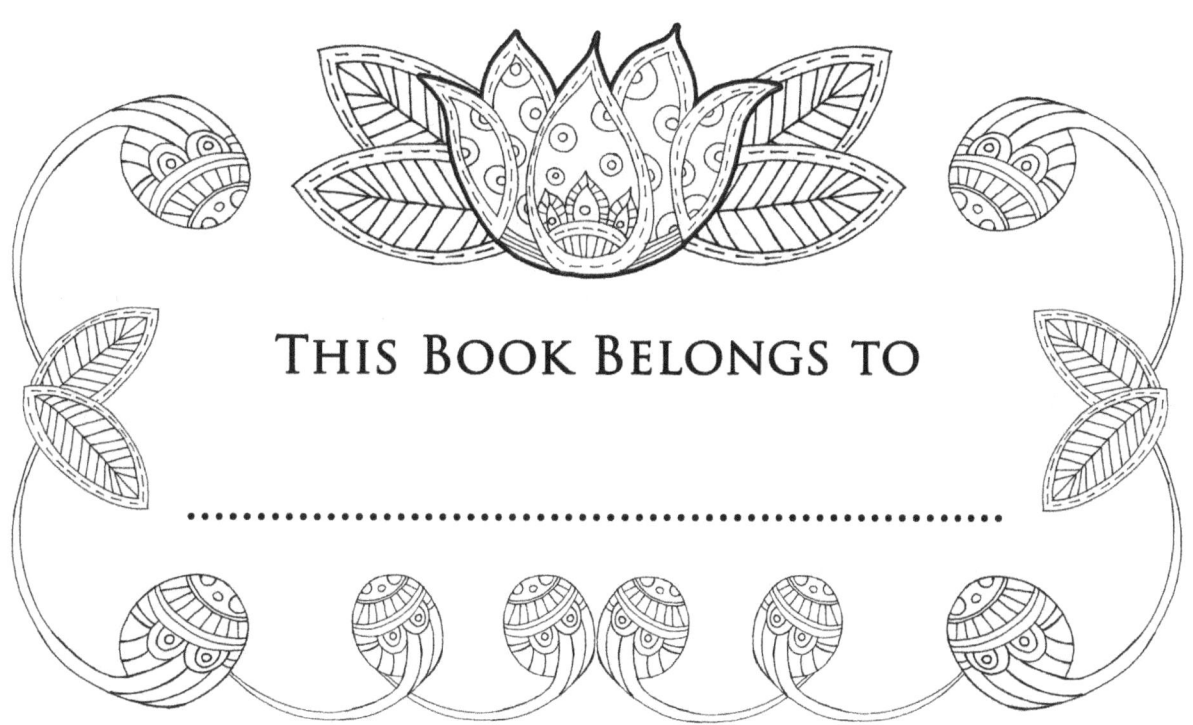

THIS BOOK BELONGS TO

....

AN ADULT COLORING BOOK

RANDOM
Quotes

T.S. DOBSON

RANDOM *Quotes*
an Adult Coloring Book

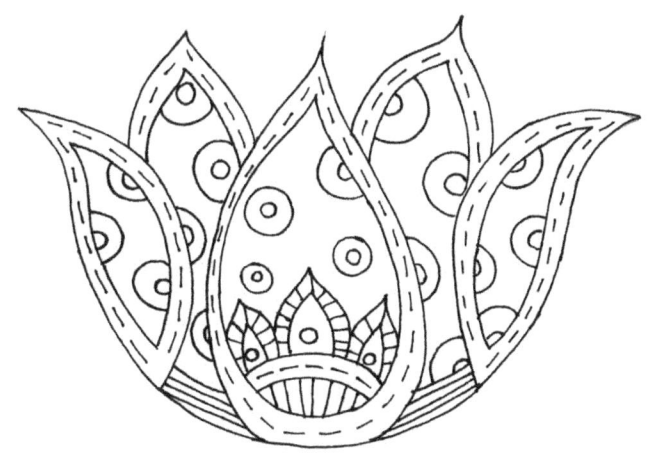

ISBN-13: 978-1533185235
ISBN-10: 1533185239

Cover and Interior Art by Teresa Scott Dobson

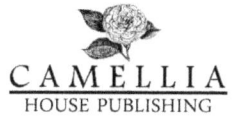

CAMELLIA
HOUSE PUBLISHING

Camellia House Publishing, Century, FL
Printed in the United States of America.

camelliahousepublishing@aol.com

RANDOM *Quotes*

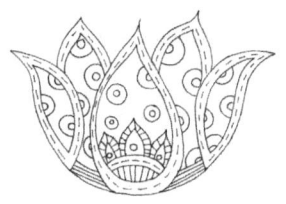

Before You Get Started!

1. Put away all of the worldly distractions around you -- TV, phone, computer, etc.
2. Take out some color pencils, markers or crayons.
3. Pick a page and go with it. There's no particular order to follow.
4. When you finish a design, personalize it by signing your name anywhere on the page.
5. Stop when you need a break, then pick it up again later.
6. When finished, if you desire, share your creations with others!

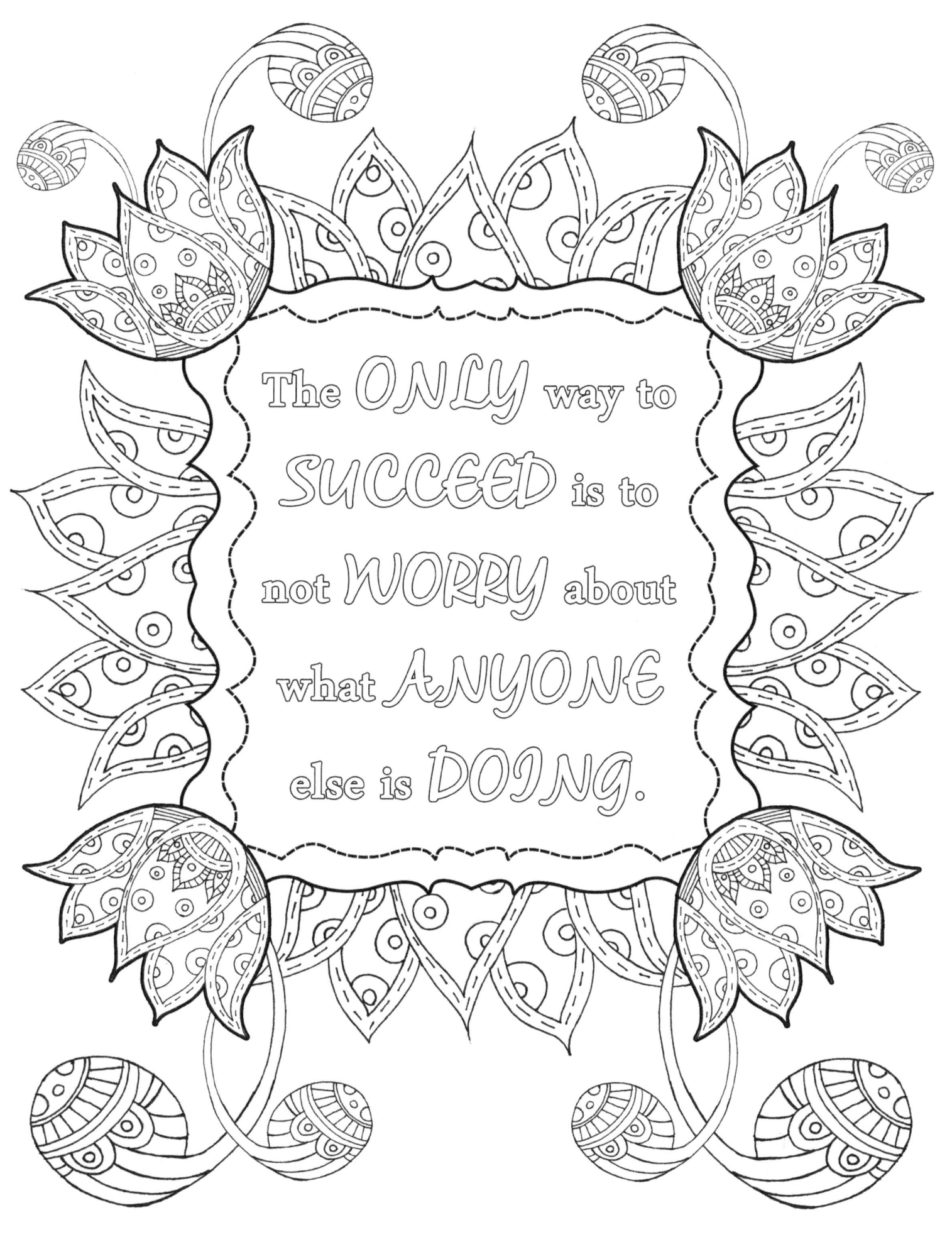

The ONLY way to SUCCEED is to not WORRY about what ANYONE else is DOING.

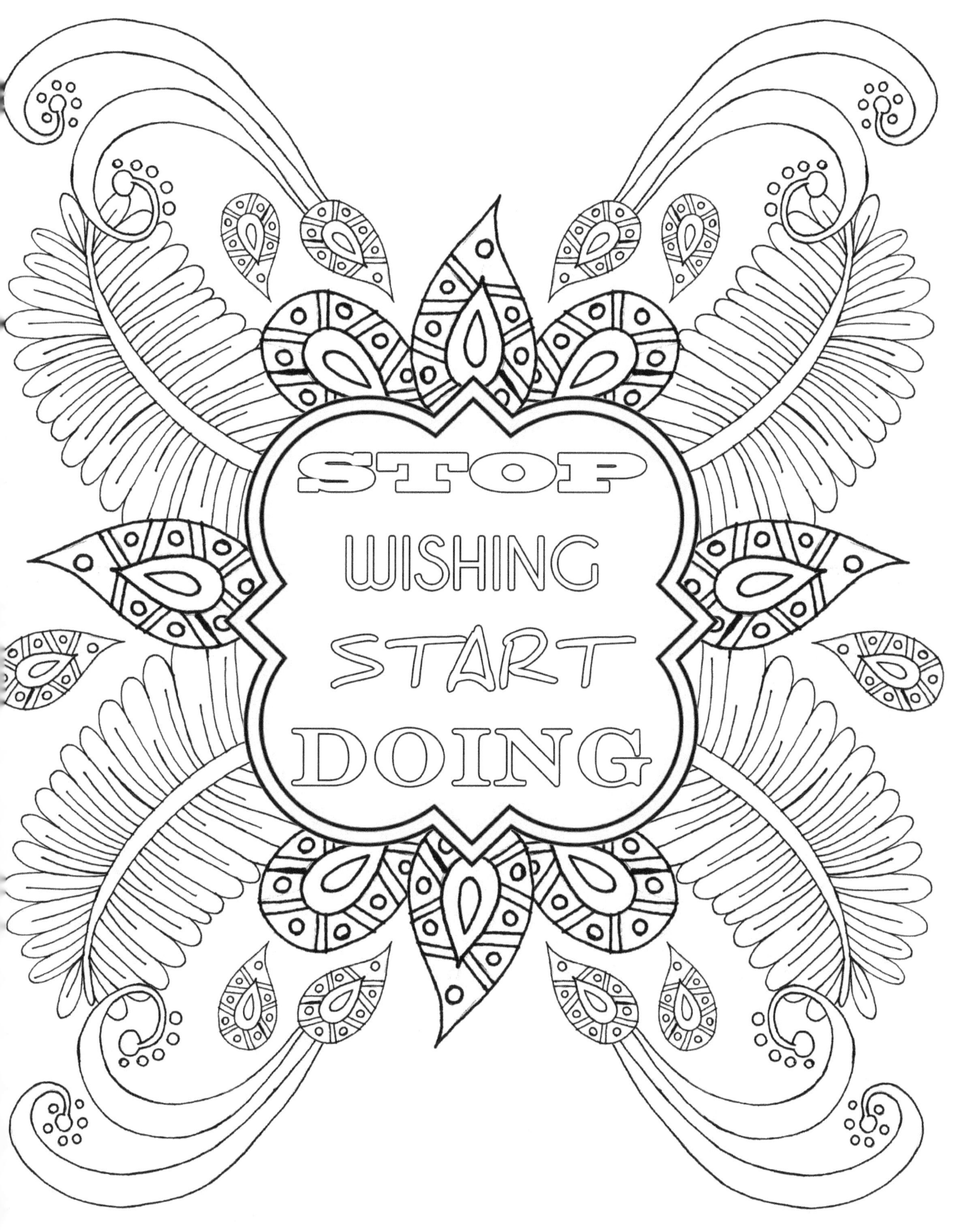

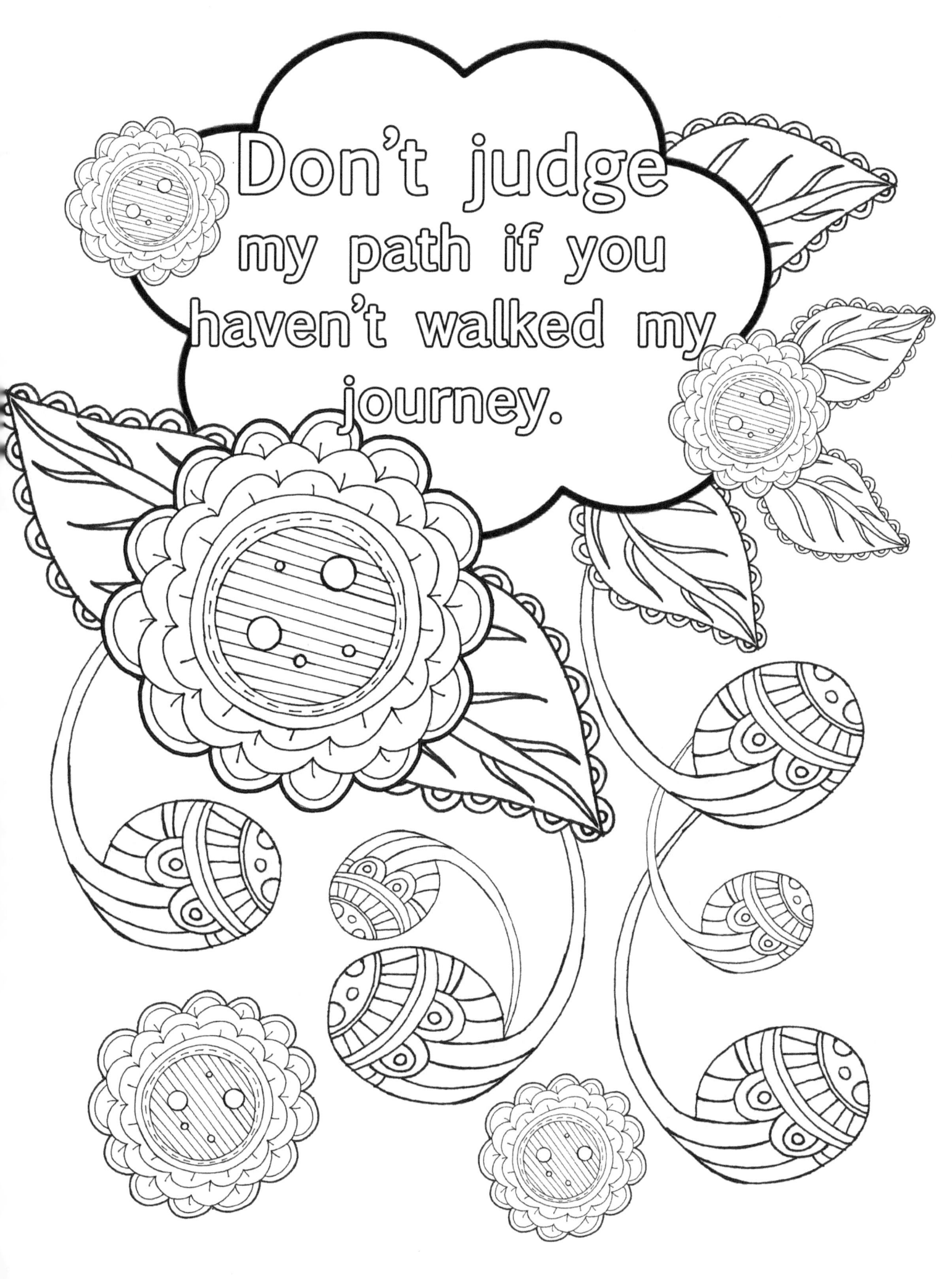

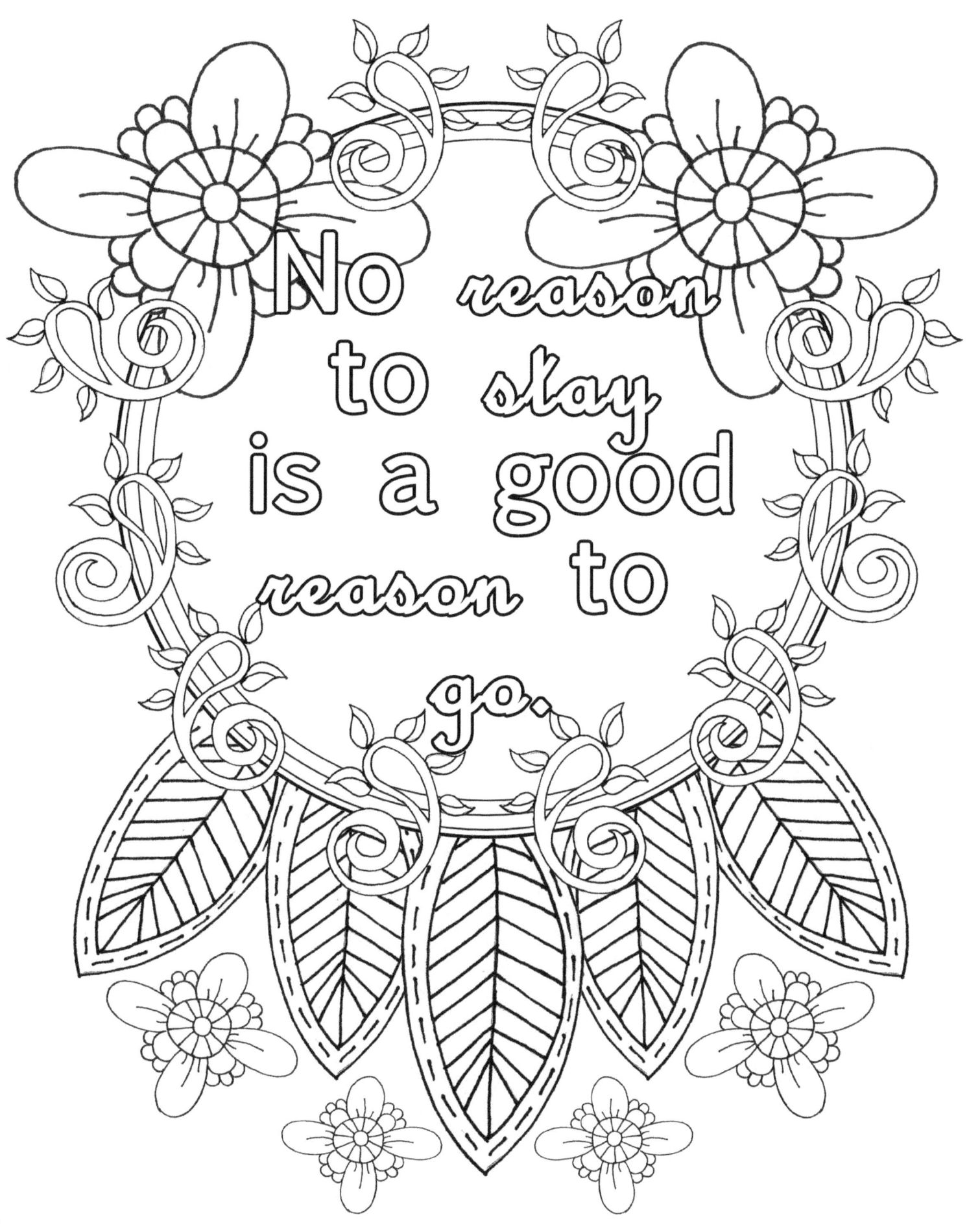

No reason to stay is a good reason to go.

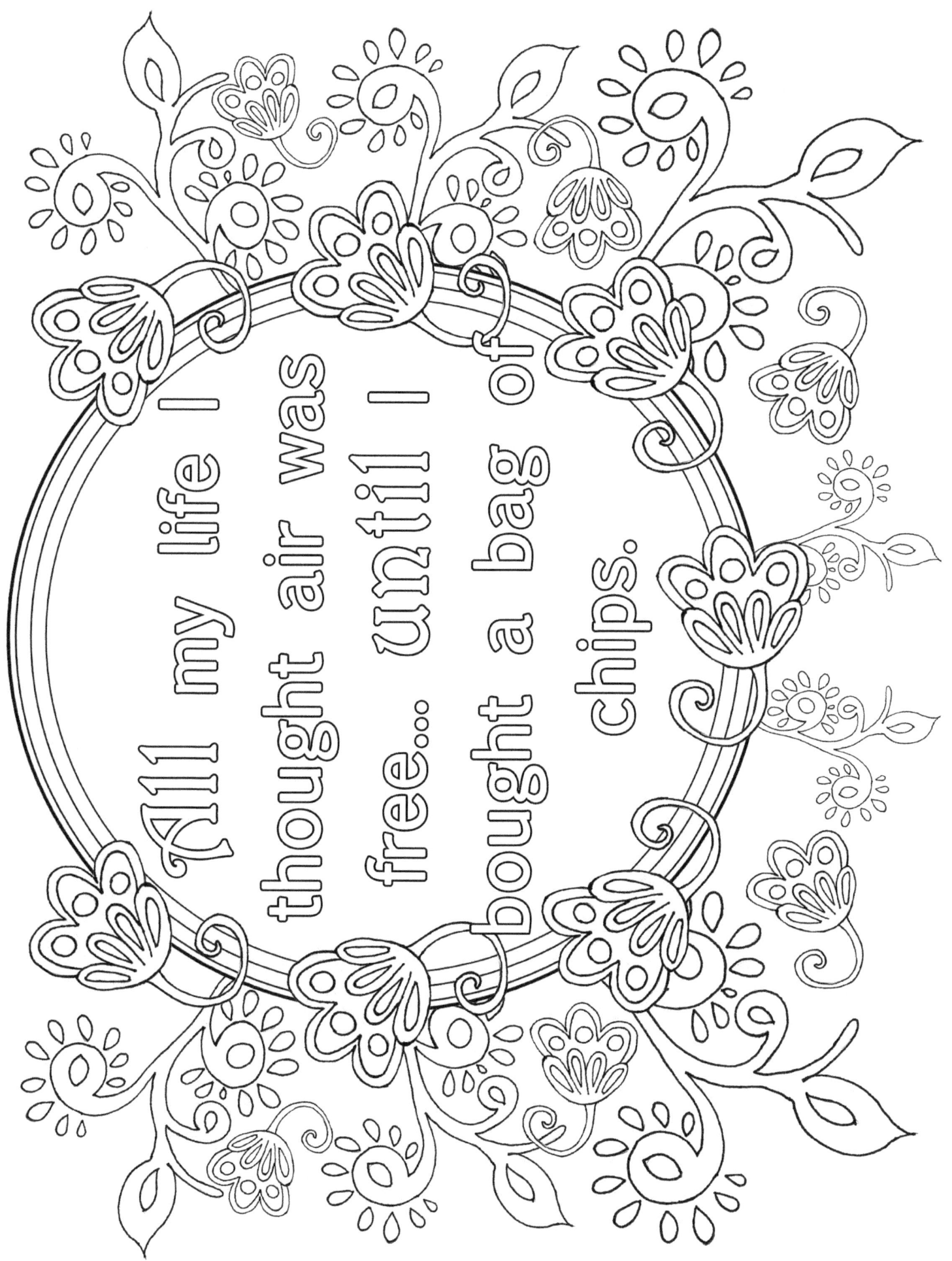

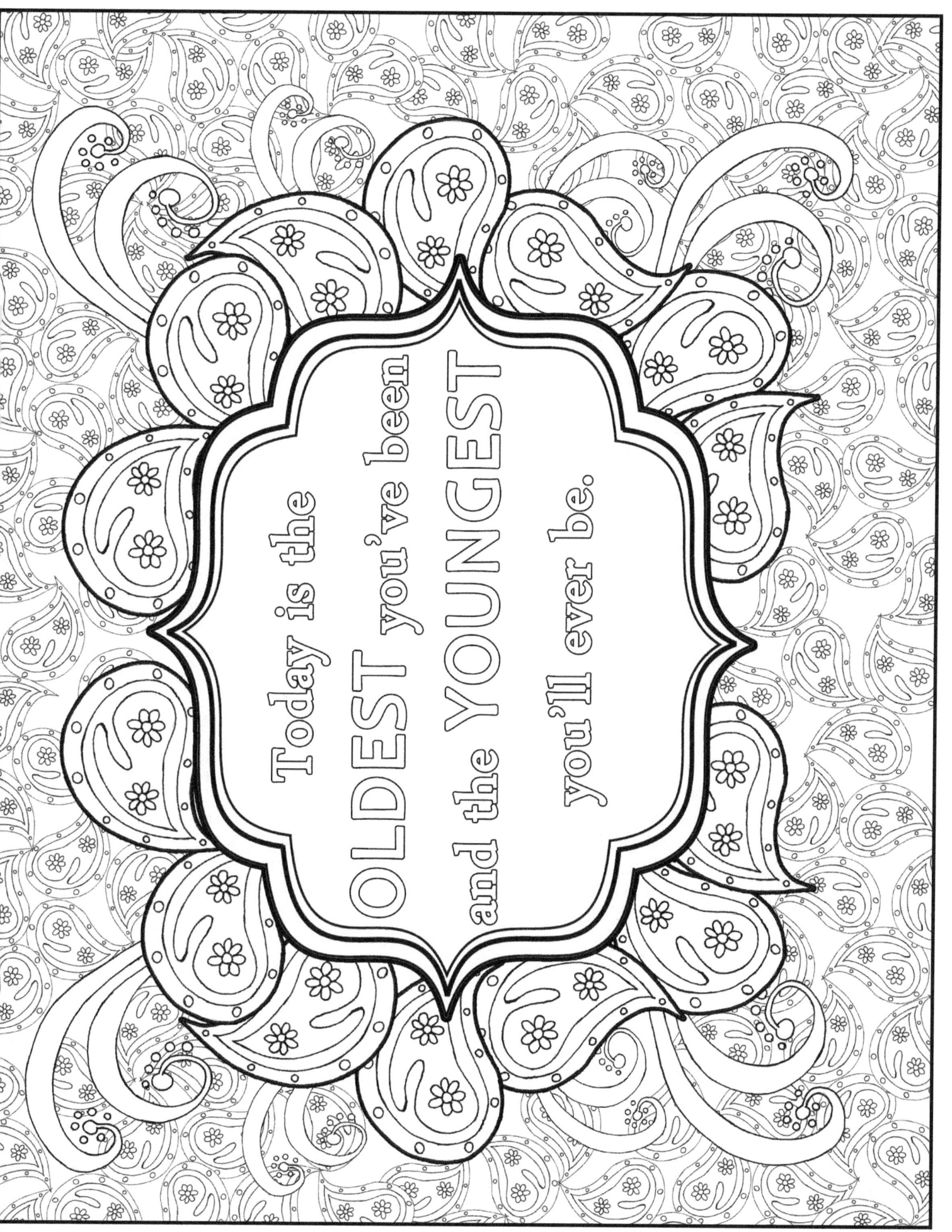

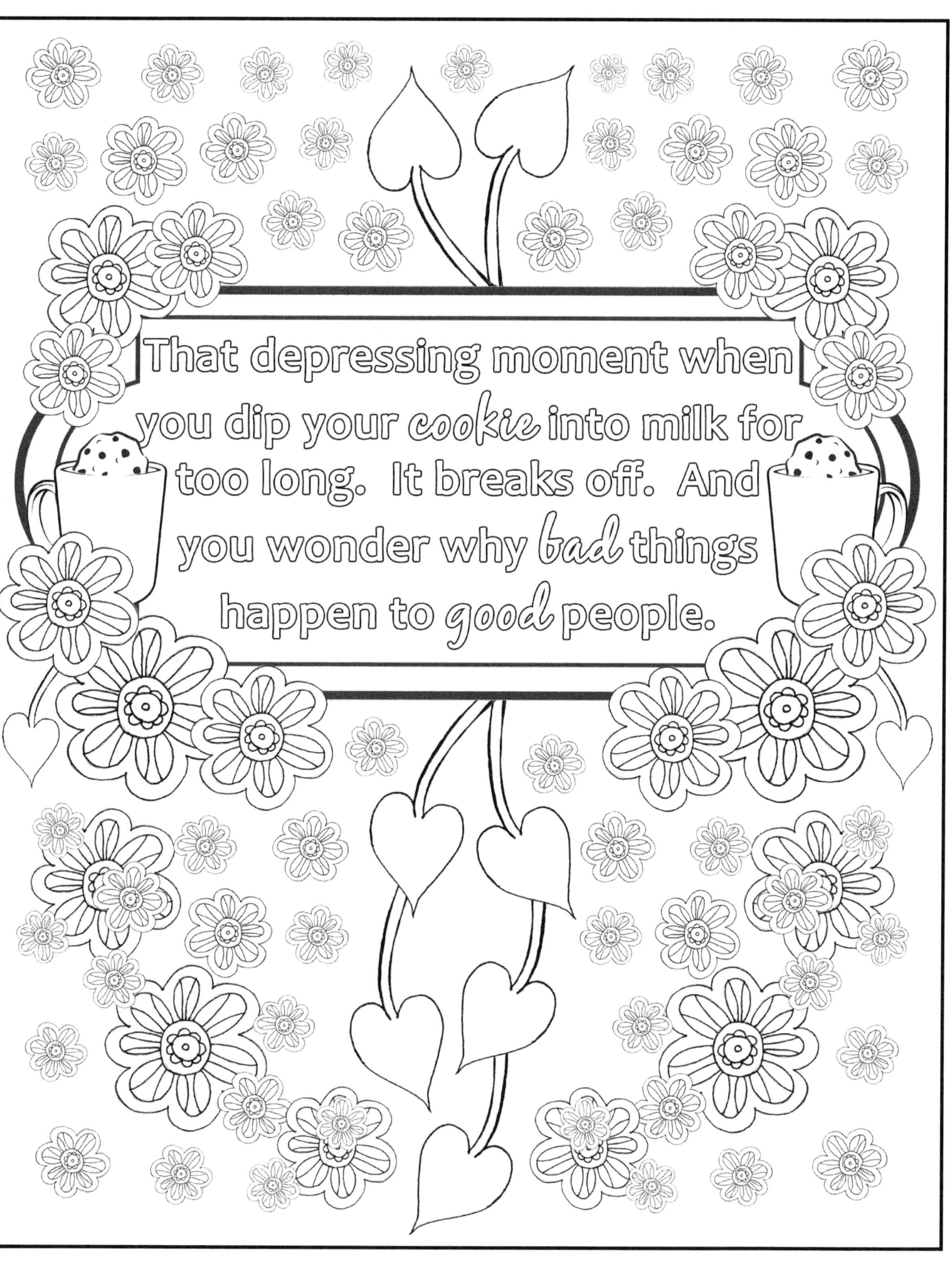

That depressing moment when you dip your *cookie* into milk for too long. It breaks off. And you wonder why *bad* things happen to *good* people.

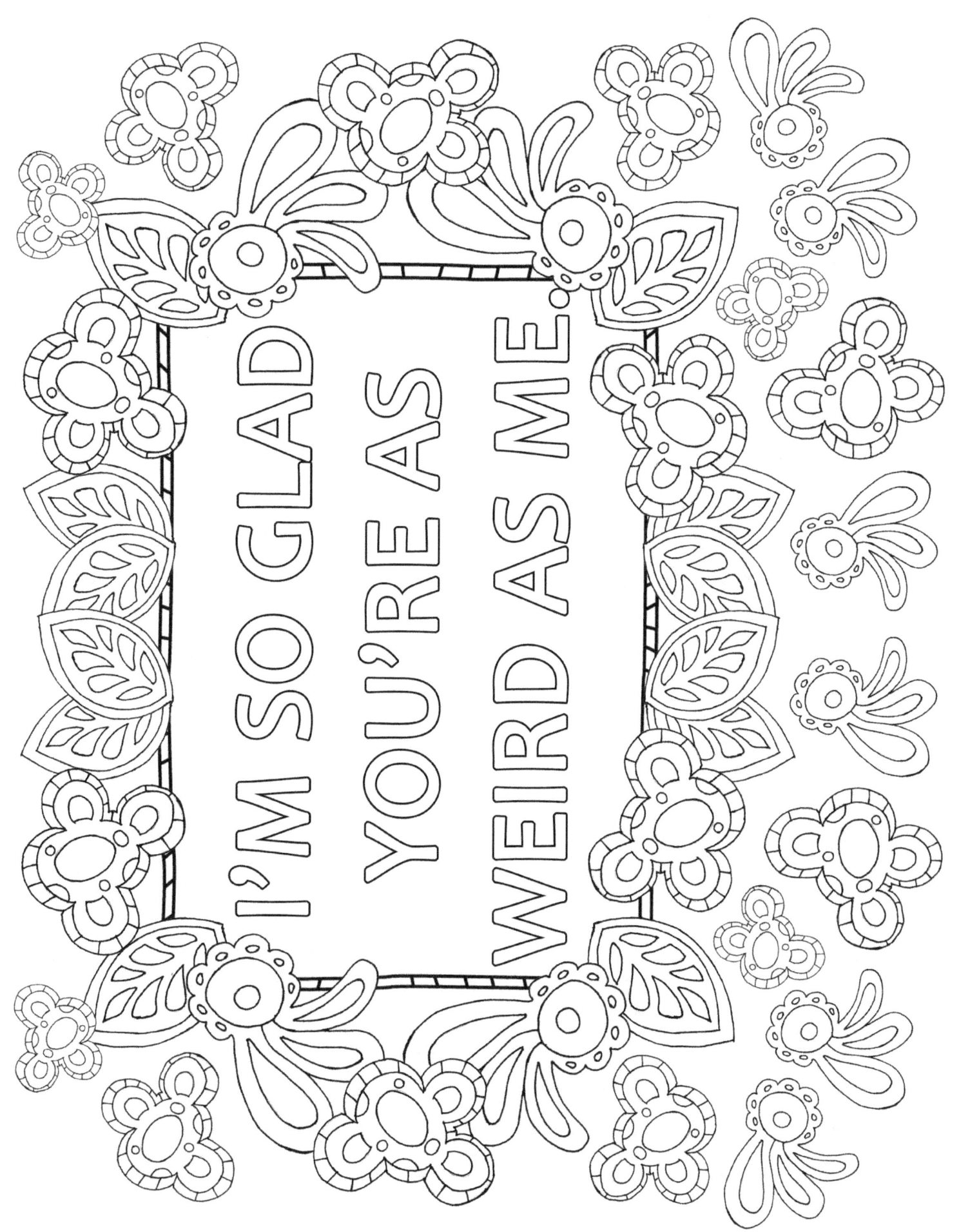

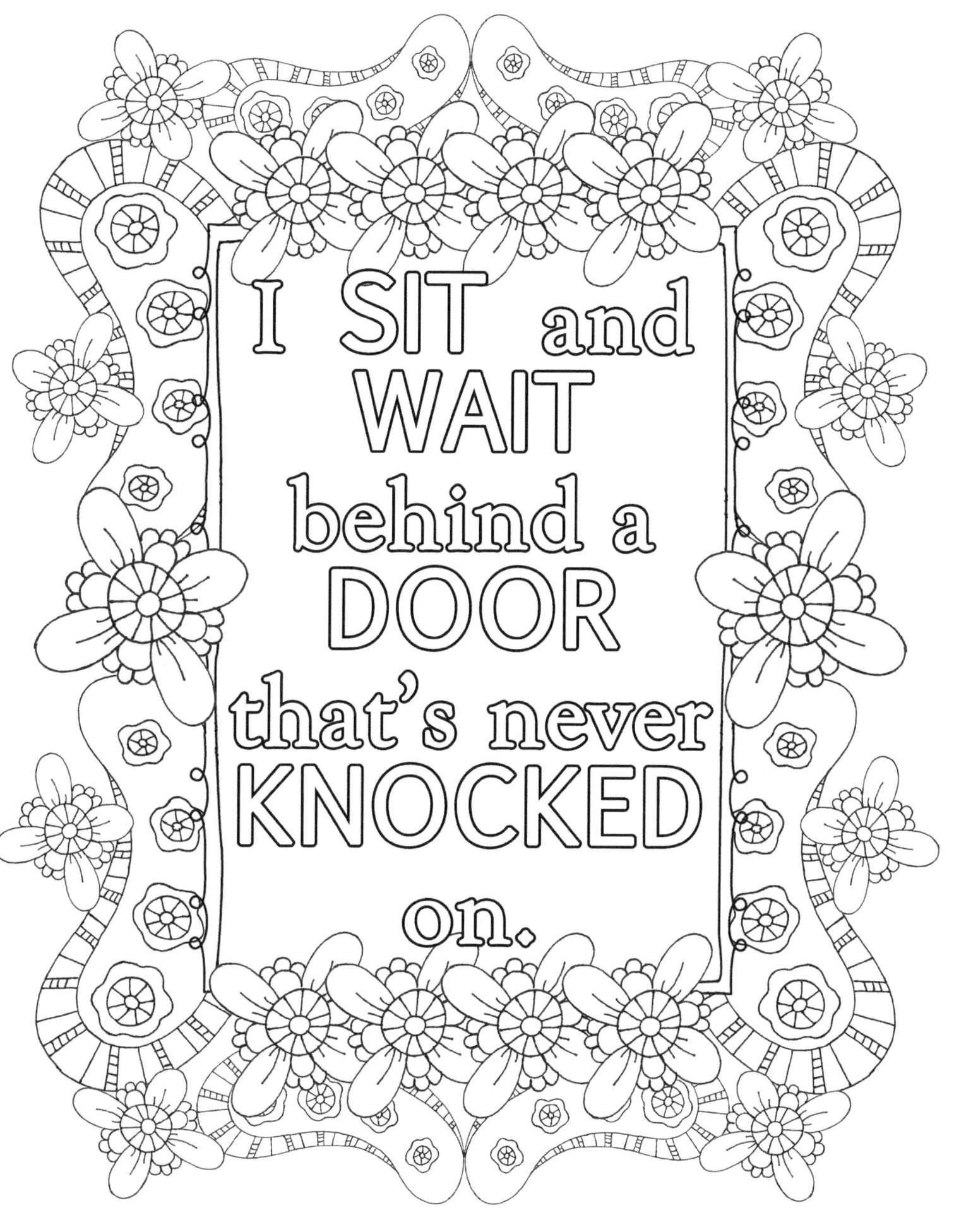

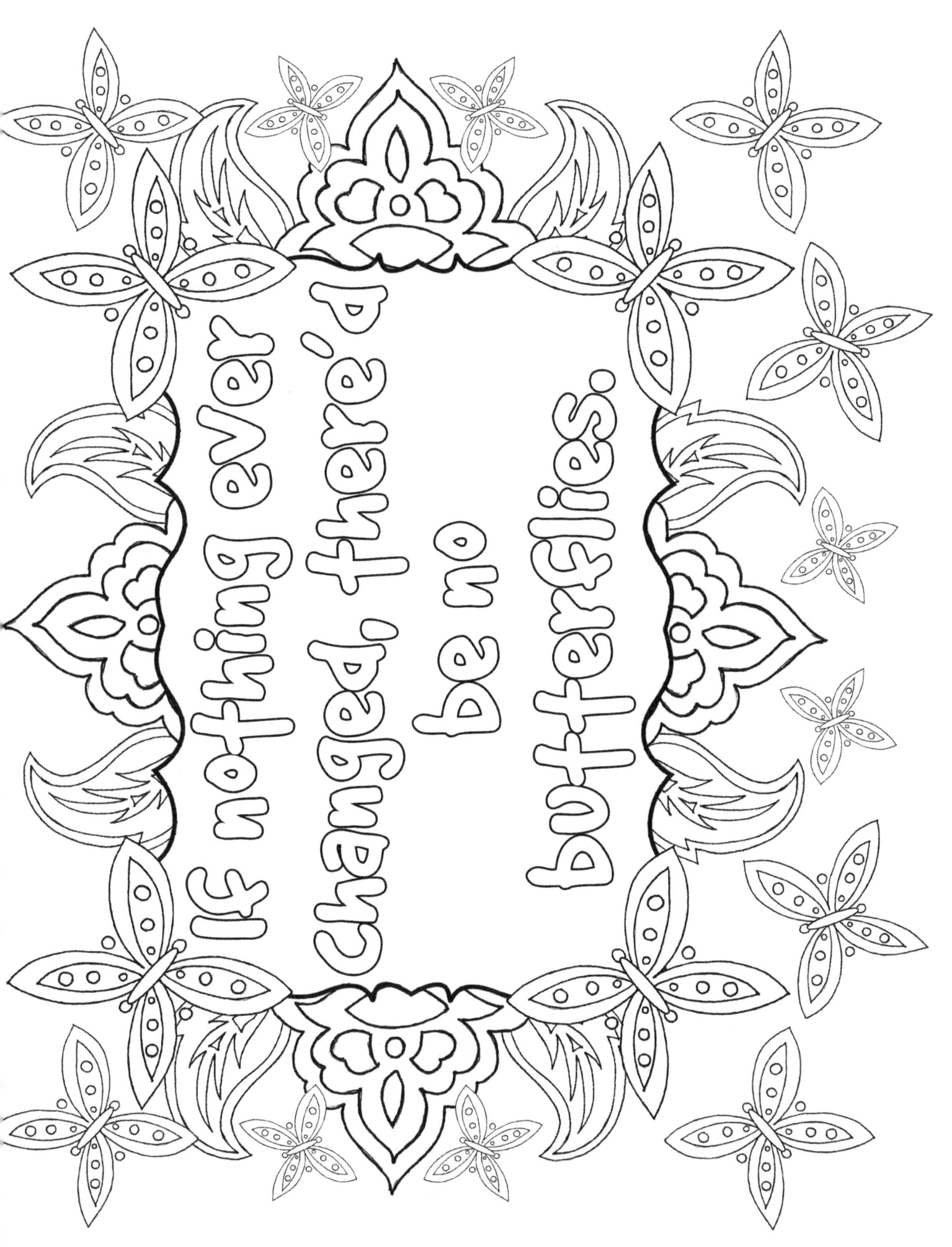

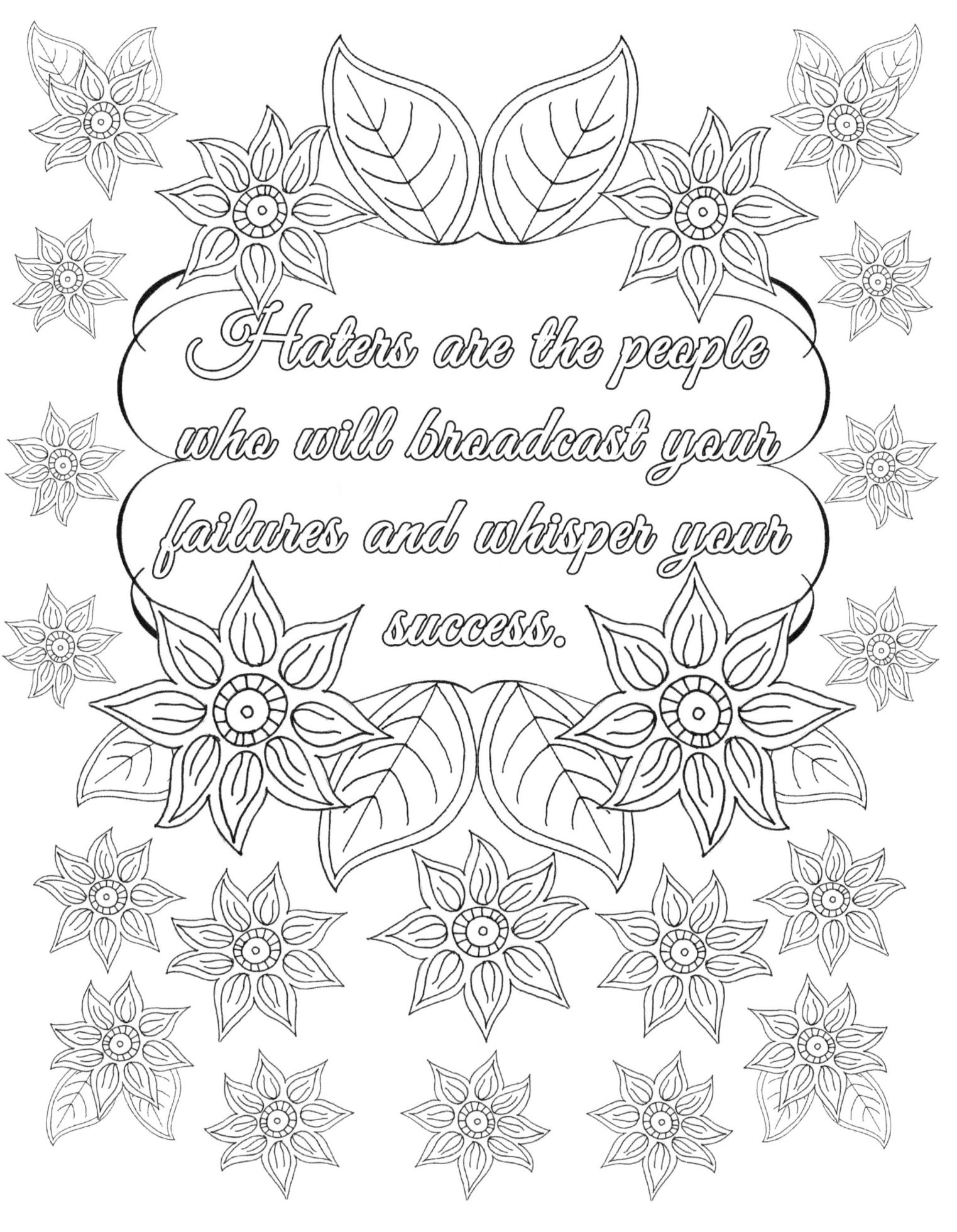

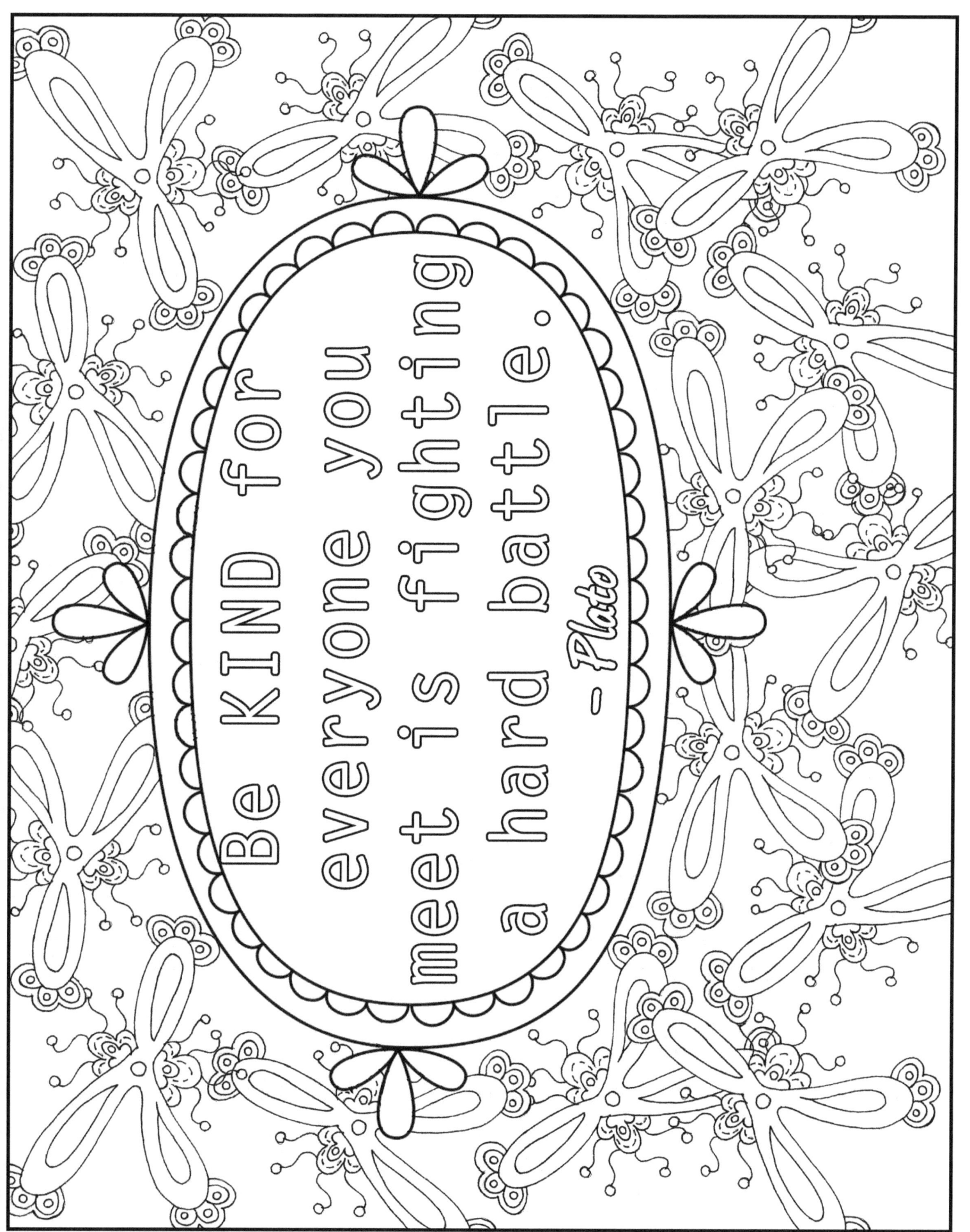

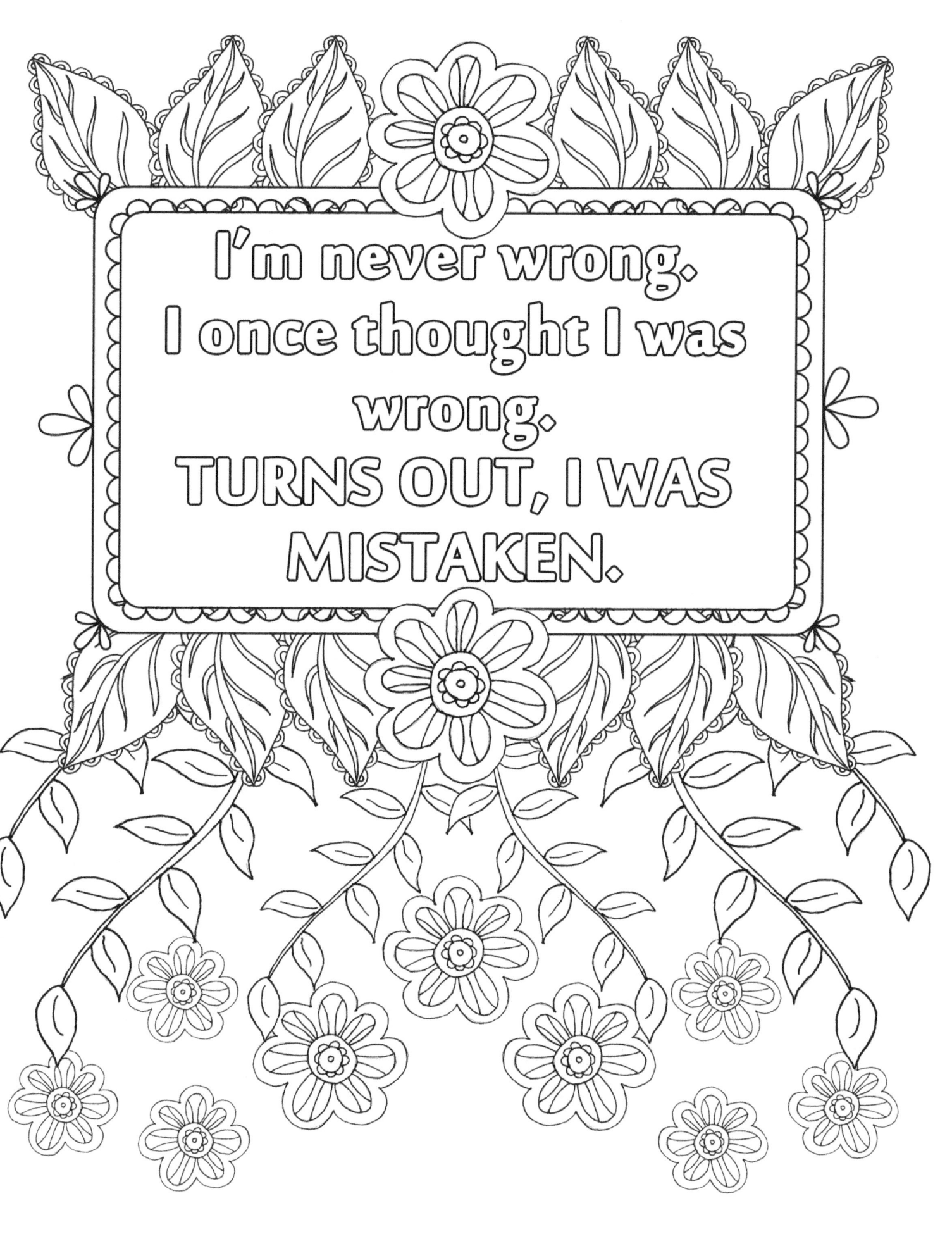

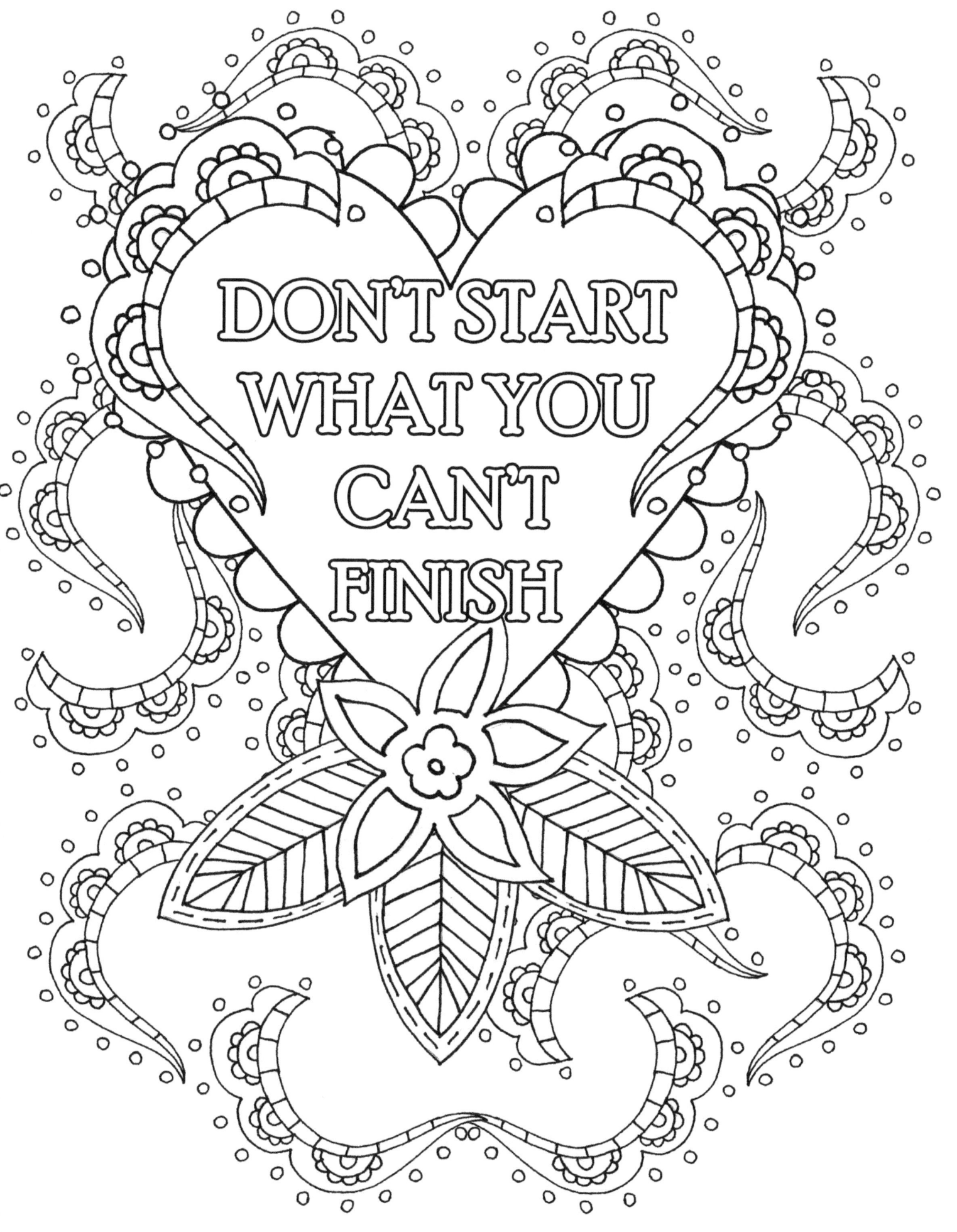

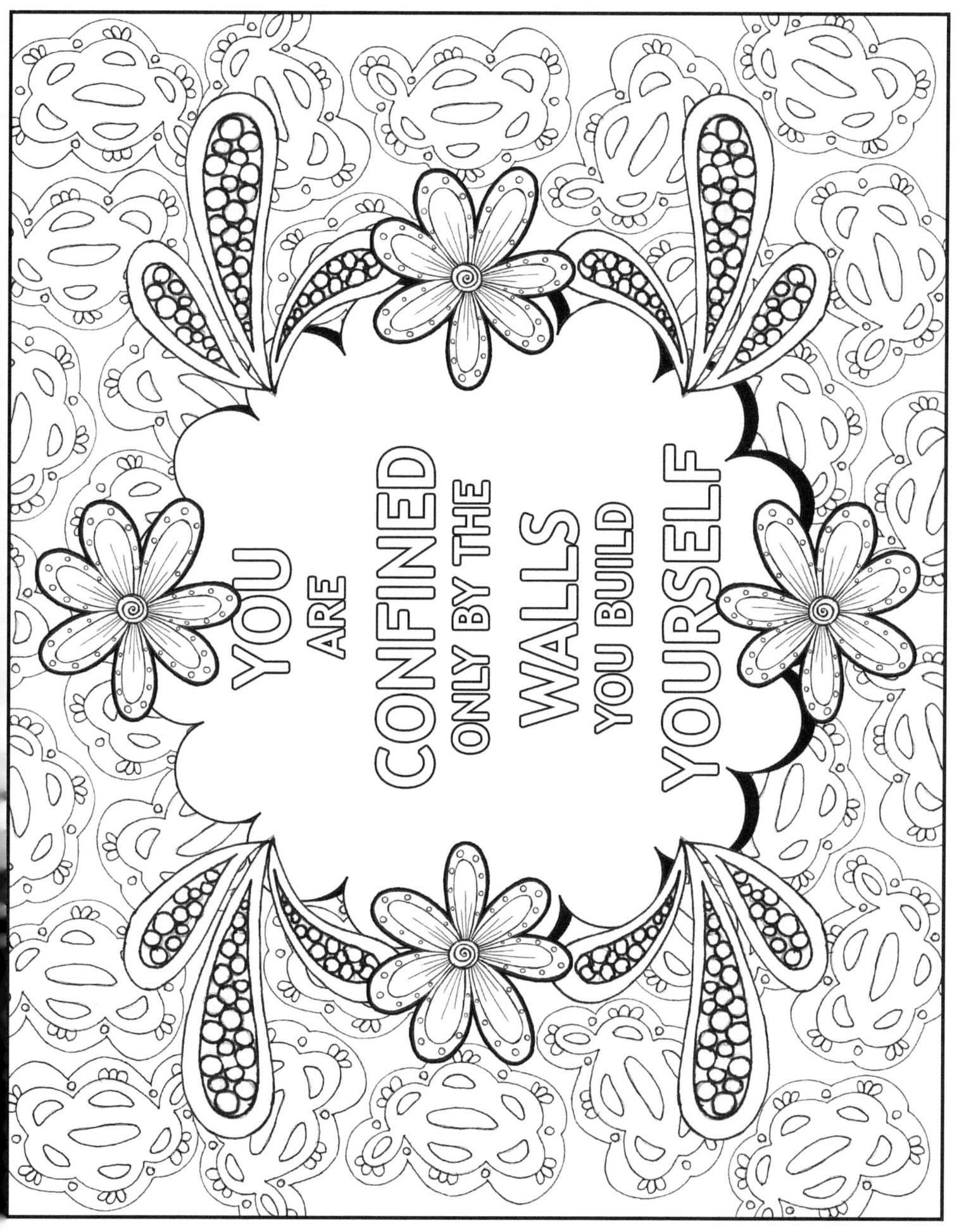

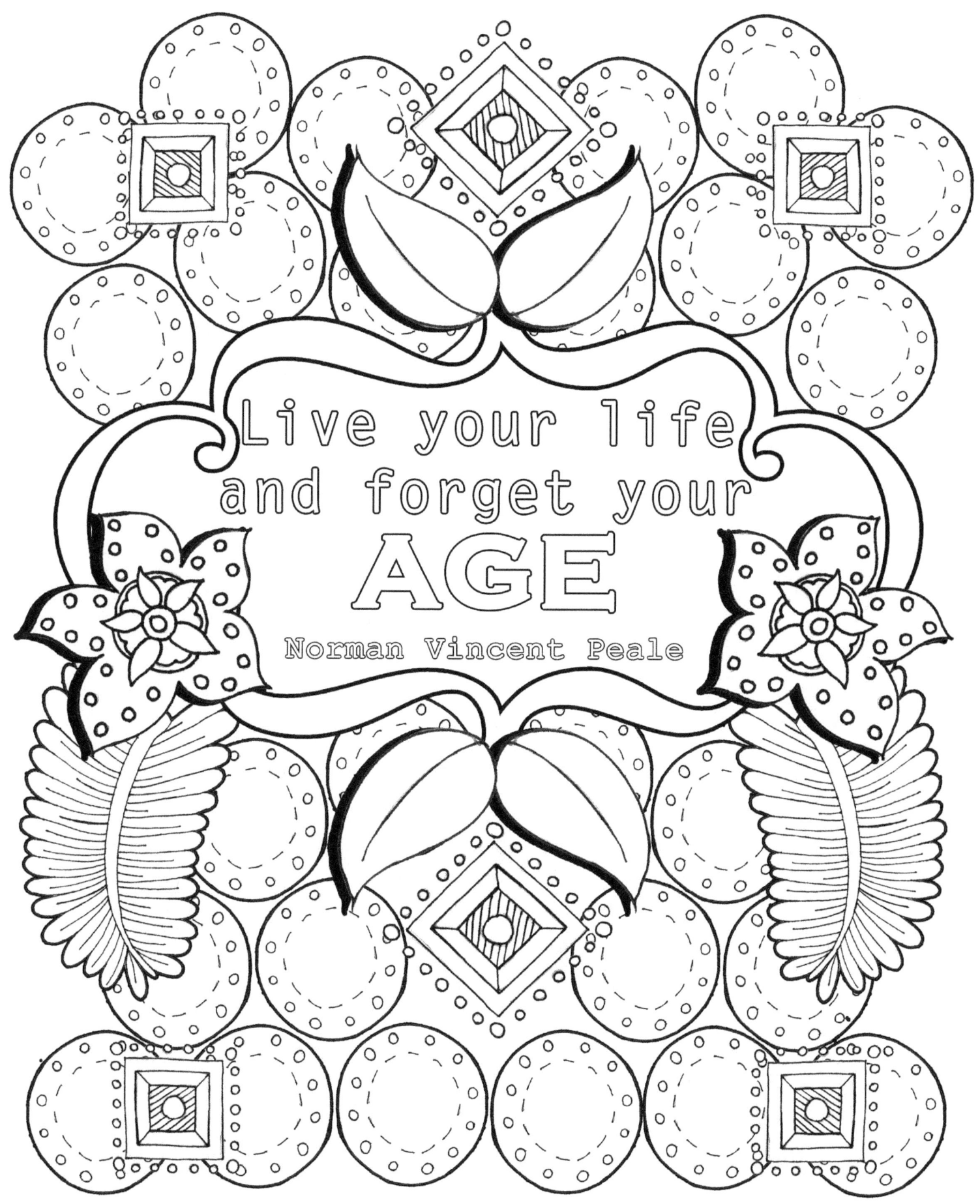

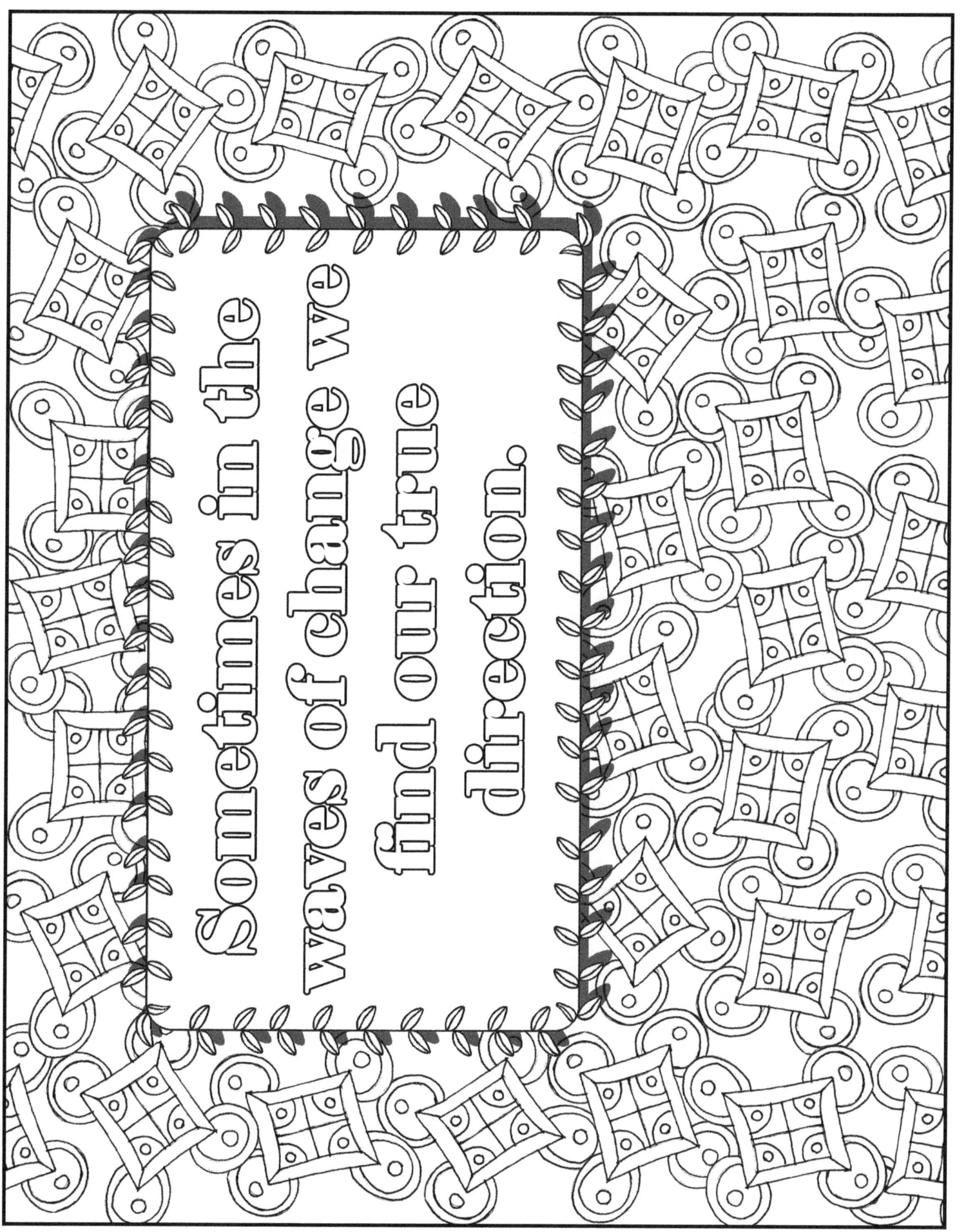

Sometimes in the waves of change we find our true direction.

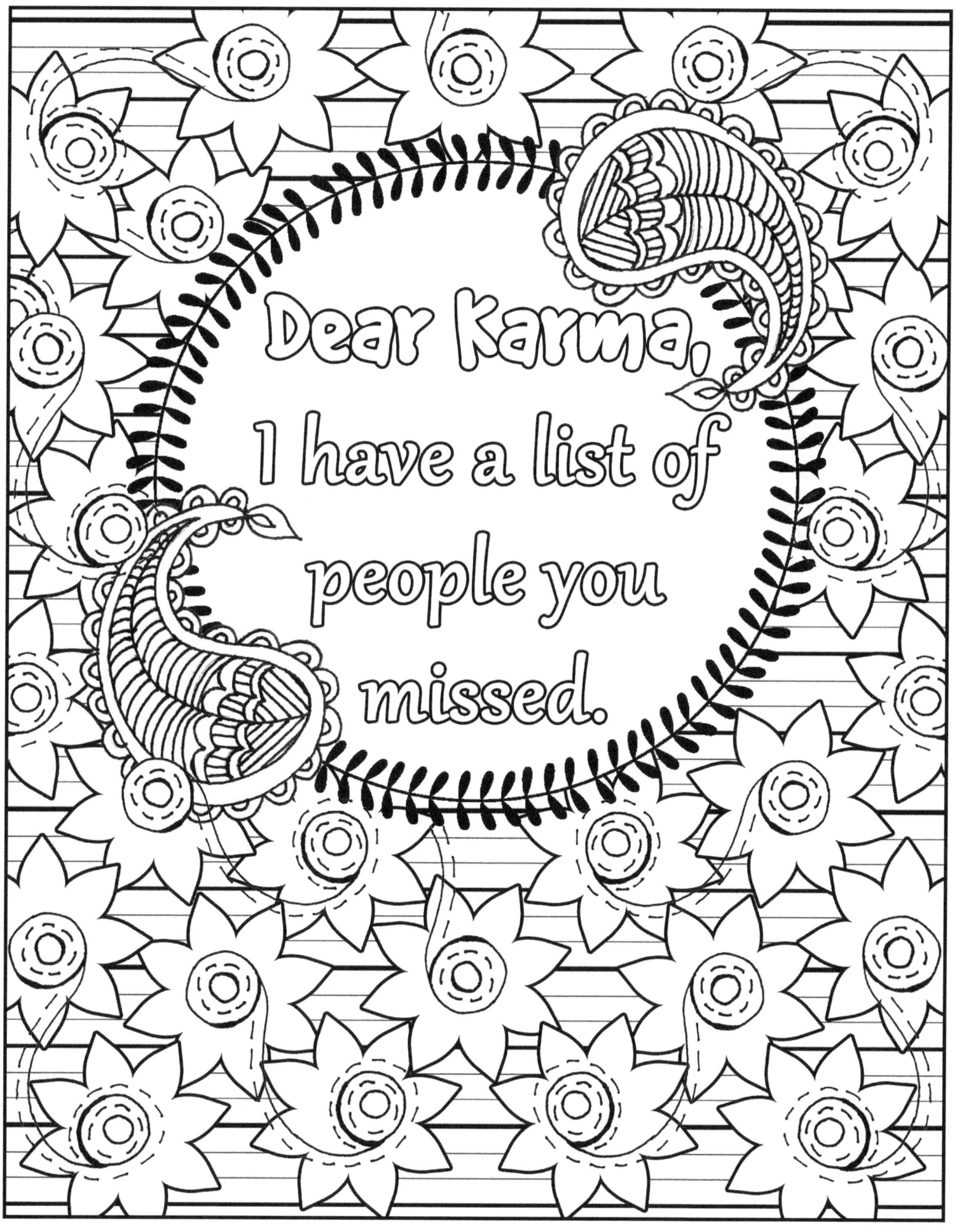

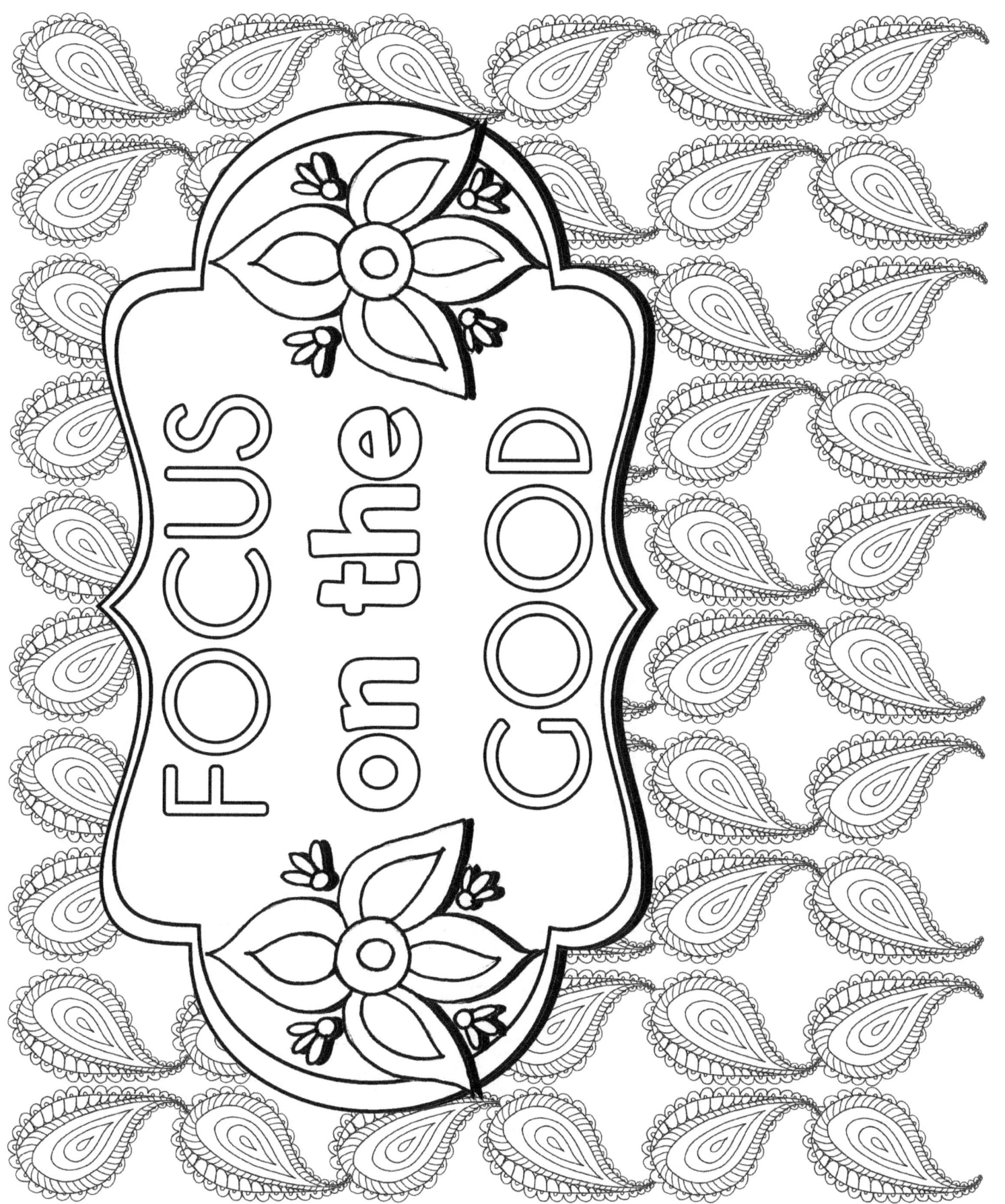

www.ingramcontent.com/pod-product-compliance
Lightning Source LLC
Chambersburg PA
CBHW080609190526
45169CB00007B/2940